Everybody is busy in the castle.

spit

The bakery

The bakers are busy.
They are baking pies and tarts.

sugar castle

The cooks are busy.

They are making a castle out of sugar.

Servants carry the food out of the kitchen, across the courtyard...

kitchen
moat
courtyard

stairs
Great Hall

up the stairs, and into the Great Hall.

The food is carried to the King.
The King's food is tasted before he eats it.

The Great Hall
striped jelly

the taster

The King's drink is tasted before he drinks it.
Someone might poison the King.

The feast begins

Everyone has a plate.

The plate is a thick slice of old bread.
The food is put on the bread.

Servants carry more food into the Great Hall.
The sugar castle is for the King.

Everyone listens to music.
Everyone watches tricks and games.

The feast ends

The feast is over.

Poor people eat the plates.
After all, the plates are made of bread.

Index